The Good Cook's Book of
DESSERTS
Carole Handslip

O9-ABE-836

CONTENTS

Fruit desserts 6

Soufflés, mousses & charlottes 22

Creamy desserts 32

Frozen desserts 42

Pies, tarts & cheesecakes 56

Puddings 66

Special occasion desserts 76

Index 94

This edition published 1982
by Octopus Books Limited
59 Grosvenor Street
London W1

© Cathay Books 1980
ISBN 0 7064 1810 7

Printed in USA

INTRODUCTION

Creating delicious desserts is fun and rewarding. Desserts often bring more compliments than the main course, so the time and effort spent on them is well worthwhile.

Choosing the right dessert to complement the meal is most important. Fresh fruity desserts are the perfect finish to a summer meal. They are usually quick to prepare and cool and refreshing to eat. Light frothy whips and soufflés are ideal to round off a rich meal. Elaborate creamy concoctions taste deliciously decadent after a lighter main course. Pies, puddings and crumbles will satisfy robust appetites, especially in the cold winter months.

Ice cream and frozen desserts are probably the most versatile of all desserts. They can, of course, be prepared well in advance and a supply in the freezer is most useful when unexpected guests arrive. They can be as light and fresh as a fruit sherbet, or as creamy rich as a Bombe au Chocolat and you will find one to suit most menus.

Most desserts can be prepared ahead of time and just need a little attention at the last minute – a point well worth remembering whether you are cooking for a hungry family or giving a dinner party.

NOTES

Standard spoon and cup measurements are used in all recipes.

All spoon and cup measures are level.

Ovens should be preheated to the specified temperature.

FRUIT DESSERTS

Tropical Fruit Salad

1 small pineapple
1 can (11 oz)
   lychees, drained
2 bananas, sliced
1 guava, peeled,
   sliced and seeds
   removed
2 passion fruit
   (optional)
1 cup ginger ale

Cut the pineapple in half lengthwise, remove the flesh and cut into pieces, discarding the center core. Place in a bowl with the lychees, bananas and guava.

Halve the passion fruit if using, scoop out the flesh and mix with the other fruits. Pour the ginger ale over and chill. Serve with cream if desired.

Serves 8

Caribbean Bananas

4 bananas, halved
  lengthwise
½ cup firmly packed
  brown sugar
2 tablespoons lemon
  juice
2 tablespoons butter
  or margarine
2 tablespoons rum

Place the bananas in an ovenproof
dish and sprinkle with the sugar and
lemon juice. Dot with the butter and
bake in a preheated 350°F oven for
15 minutes.

Arrange the bananas on a warmed
serving plate and spoon the sauce
over.

Warm the rum, pour over the
bananas and carefully ignite. Serve
flaming, with cream if desired.
Serves 4

Peaches in Blackberry Sauce

1 can (15¾ oz)
   blackberries
¼ cup sugar
¼ cup water
grated rind and juice
   of 1 orange
6 ripe peaches,
   peeled

Place the blackberries with their juice in a saucepan. Add the sugar and water and heat, stirring, until the sugar dissolves. Cool slightly, then process in a blender or food processor. Strain, discarding the seeds. Add the orange rind and juice.

Place the peaches in a serving bowl and pour the blackberry sauce over. Chill, and serve with cream if desired.
Serves 6

Swedish Strawberry Surprise

MERINGUE:
2 egg whites
½ cup sugar
FILLING:
½ cup sugar
⅔ cup water
1 pint strawberries
3 envelopes (3 tablespoons) unflavored gelatin, soaked in ¼ cup cold water
¾ cup heavy cream, whipped with 2 tablespoons sugar
grated chocolate to decorate

To make the meringue, beat the egg whites until stiff. Beat in 3 tablespoons of the sugar. Fold in the remainder.

Spoon the meringue into a pastry bag fitted with a ¼ inch plain tip and pipe tiny mounds onto a cookie sheet lined with parchment paper. Bake in a preheated 300°F oven for 1½ to 2 hours.

For the filling, place the sugar and water in a saucepan. Heat, stirring, until dissolved. Add the strawberries and cook gently for 15 minutes. Process in a blender or food processor.

Place the gelatin in a bowl over a pan of simmering water and stir until dissolved. Add to the strawberry purée and let stand until almost set, stirring occasionally. Pour into a dampened 1½ quart soufflé dish and place in the refrigerator to set.

Invert onto a plate. Spread the whipped cream over the top and sides and decorate with the meringues. Sprinkle with chocolate.
Serves 6

Apricot Delight

3 tablespoons butter
  or margarine
½ cup firmly packed
  brown sugar
1 can (16 oz) apricot
  halves
2 ripe bananas, sliced
grated rind and juice
  of 1 lemon
½ teaspoon ground
  cinnamon
TO SERVE:
vanilla ice cream or
  Crémets (see page
  15)

Spread 1½ tablespoons of the butter in a 9 inch square baking pan. Sprinkle with ¼ cup of the brown sugar. Drain the apricots, reserving ¼ cup of the juice. Arrange the apricots, cut sides down, around the inside edge of the pan. Place the banana slices in the center of the pan. Sprinkle with the lemon rind and juice and cinnamon. Pour the reserved apricot juice over the fruit and sprinkle with the remaining ¼ cup brown sugar. Dot the top with the remaining 1½ tablespoons of butter.

Bake in a preheated 375°F oven for 30 minutes. Spoon onto individual serving dishes and serve with vanilla ice cream or Crémets.
Serves 4

Apple Mold

¾ cup sugar
6 tablespoons water
grated rind and juice
  of 1 lemon
2 lb apples, peeled
  and cored
¼ cup chopped glacé
  cherries
¼ cup chopped
  preserved ginger
YOGURT SAUCE:
¾ cup heavy cream
½ cup plain yogurt
2 tablespoons sugar

Place the sugar, water and lemon rind and juice in a saucepan and heat gently, stirring, until dissolved. Bring to a boil and boil for 5 minutes.

Thinly slice the apples into the syrup. Cover and simmer gently for 10 minutes, turning the apples once carefully. Remove the cover and simmer until most of the syrup has evaporated.

Add the cherries and ginger to the pan, cover and let cool.

Spoon the mixture into a dampened 1½ quart soufflé dish and chill in the refrigerator overnight.

To make the sauce, whip the cream until it holds its shape, then fold in the yogurt and sugar.

Invert the apple mold onto a plate and serve with the sauce.
Serves 6

Apple Snow

*1 lb apples, peeled
  and cored*
¼ cup sugar
3 tablespoons water
2 egg whites
*grated rind and juice
  of ½ lemon*
lady fingers to serve

Slice the apples into a saucepan,
sprinkle with the sugar and add the
water. Cover and simmer gently for
10 to 15 minutes. Cool slightly, then
process in a blender or food
processor until smooth. Let cool.

Beat the egg whites until stiff and
fold into the apple purée with the
lemon rind and juice.

Spoon into champagne glasses and
serve with lady fingers.
Serves 4

11

Baked Apples with Dates

4 large apples
1/4 cup chopped dates
1/4 cup raisins
1/4 cup firmly packed
  brown sugar
1/2 teaspoon ground
  cinnamon
1 tablespoon butter or
  margarine

Remove the cores from the apples.
Make a cut around the middle of
each apple.

Mix together the dates, raisins,
sugar and cinnamon and fill the
apples.

Place in a baking dish and dot each
apple with a little butter. Bake in a
preheated 350°F oven for 50 to 60
minutes or until tender. Serve hot
with cream.

Serves 4

Apple Amber

1 lb apples, peeled
   and cored
1 tablespoon water
¼ cup sugar
2 egg yolks
grated rind and juice
   of ½ lemon
MERINGUE:
2 egg whites
½ cup sugar

Slice the apples into a saucepan and add the water and sugar. Cover and cook gently until very soft, stirring occasionally. Remove from the heat and beat until smooth. Beat in the egg yolks and lemon rind and juice and pour into a 2½ cup baking dish.

To make the meringue, beat the egg whites until stiff. Beat in 2 tablespoons of the sugar, then fold in the remainder. Spoon the meringue on top of the apple mixture and swirl into peaks.

Bake in a preheated 325°F oven for 20 to 30 minutes or until golden. Serve hot or cold.

Serves 4

13

Calvados Apples

½ cup sugar
1¼ cups water
6 apples, peeled and
    quartered
¼ cup Calvados or
    brandy
CARAMEL:
⅓ cup sugar
¼ cup water
TO SERVE:
lace roll-ups

Place the sugar and water in a
saucepan and heat gently, stirring,
until the sugar dissolves. Bring to a
boil, then simmer for 5 minutes.
Place the apples in the syrup, cover
and simmer for 15 to 20 minutes. Let
cool. Remove the apples to a glass
serving dish.

Boil the syrup rapidly until
reduced by about half, then add the
Calvados or brandy. Pour over the
apples. Let cool.

To make the caramel, place the
sugar and water in a saucepan and
heat gently, stirring, until dissolved,
then boil rapidly until golden brown.
Pour onto an oiled cookie sheet and
let harden. When set, crack into
pieces and sprinkle over the apples.
Serve with lace roll-ups.
Serves 4

Red Fruit Compote

1 cup sugar
1¼ cups water
1 lb dark cherries,
    pitted
grated rind and juice
    of ½ orange
1 pint strawberries
1 pint blackberries
1 pint raspberries
1½ tablespoons
    arrowroot
2 tablespoons port
Crémets (see page
    15) to serve

Place the sugar and water in a
saucepan and heat gently, stirring,
until the sugar dissolves. Bring to a
boil and boil for a few minutes, then
add the cherries and orange rind.
Simmer gently for 5 minutes or until
soft.

Drain the cherries, reserving the
syrup. Place the cherries in a serving
dish and add the remaining fruit.

Return the syrup to the saucepan
and bring to a boil. Mix the
arrowroot with the orange juice and
stir into the boiling syrup. Cook,
stirring, until thickened. Add the
port and pour over the fruit. Allow
to cool before serving, with crémets.
Serves 8

Crémets

1 cup cream-style
    cottage cheese
2 tablespoons sugar
1 cup heavy cream

Combine the cheese with the sugar,
then gradually beat in the cream.
Spoon into a serving dish and chill.
Serve with stewed fruit.
Serves 4 to 6

15

Winter Fruit Salad

2½ cups water
2 tablespoons honey
1 inch piece of
cinnamon stick
2 cloves
juice of ½ lemon
1 cup dried apricots,
soaked overnight
¾ cup prunes,
soaked overnight
¾ cup dried figs,
soaked overnight
½ cup raisins
¼ cup coarsely
chopped walnuts
2 tablespoons sliced
almonds, toasted

Place the water, honey, cinnamon stick and cloves in a saucepan and bring to a boil. Add the lemon juice. Drain the dried fruits and add to the pan. Cover and simmer gently for 10 minutes.

Add the raisins and simmer for 2 to 3 minutes. Discard the cinnamon stick.

Spoon into individual serving dishes and sprinkle with the walnuts and almonds. Serve warm or cold, with cream if desired.

Serves 6

Fruit Chartreuse

3¼ cups water
1 cup sugar
thinly pared rind and
  juice of 3 lemons
1 inch piece of
  cinnamon stick
3 envelopes (3
  tablespoons)
  unflavored gelatin,
  soaked in ½ cup
  water
¼ cup sherry
½ lb black grapes,
  seeded
½ lb seedless grapes
¾ cup heavy cream,
  whipped with 2
  tablespoons sugar

Place the water, sugar, lemon rind
and juice and cinnamon stick in a
saucepan. Heat gently, stirring, until
the sugar has dissolved. Add the
gelatin mixture and stir until
dissolved. Add the sherry and allow
to cool slightly. Discard the lemon
rind and cinnamon stick.

Pour a little of the mixture into a
5 cup ring mold and refrigerate until
set. Arrange some of the black
grapes on the set gelatin, pour
enough gelatin over to cover and
refrigerate until set. Add another
layer of gelatin and let set, then
arrange green grapes on top.
Continue in this way until the mold
is full; refrigerate until set.

Invert onto a serving dish and
decorate with piped whipped cream
and any remaining grapes.
Serves 8 to 10

Pineapple Boats

1 large pineapple
1/2 cup confectioners
  sugar, sifted
grated rind of
  1/2 orange
1/4 cup Curaçao or
  Cointreau
1 pint strawberries
1 1/2 cups heavy
  cream
1/4 cup sugar

Cut the pineapple in half lengthwise,
scoop out the flesh, discarding the
central core, and cut into cubes.
Reserve the shells. Place the cubes in
a bowl with the confectioners sugar
and orange rind. Pour the Curaçao
over and let soak for 2 hours.

Set aside a few strawberries for
decoration; slice the remainder.
Whip the cream with the sugar until
stiff, then fold in the sliced
strawberries and the pineapple
mixture.

Spoon into the pineapple shells,
decorate with the reserved
strawberries and refrigerate for 30
minutes before serving.
Serves 4 to 6

Pavlova

4 egg whites
1 cup sugar
1 tablespoon
  cornstarch
2 teaspoons white
  vinegar
1/4 teaspoon vanilla
FILLING:
1 1/2 cups heavy cream
1/4 cup sugar
2 bananas, sliced
1 small pineapple,
  cut into cubes
2 peaches, peeled and
  sliced
2 passion fruit,
  peeled and sliced
  (optional)

Beat the egg whites until foamy.
Add the sugar, a little at a time,
beating until the meringue is very
stiff. Beat in the cornstarch, vinegar
and vanilla.

Spoon the meringue onto a cookie
sheet lined with parchment paper and
spread into a 9 inch round. Hollow
out the center slightly and bake in a
preheated 300°F oven for 1 1/2 hours.

Cool, then remove from the paper
and place on a serving plate. Whip
the cream with the sugar until stiff
and fold in some of the fruit. Spoon
into the meringue and decorate with
the remaining fruit.
Serves 6 to 8

Pears in Red Wine

²/₃ cup sugar
²/₃ cup water
²/₃ cup dry red wine
1 inch piece of
  cinnamon stick
6 bosc pears
2 teaspoons
  arrowroot

Place the sugar, water, wine and cinnamon stick in a saucepan. Heat gently until the sugar has dissolved. Bring to a boil and boil for 5 minutes.

Peel the pears, leaving on the stems, and place in the syrup. Cover and simmer for 20 to 30 minutes or until tender. Discard the cinnamon stick. Arrange the pears in a serving dish.

Mix the arrowroot with a little water, then add to the syrup and bring to a boil, stirring constantly. Simmer, stirring, for 1 minute. Let cool, then spoon over the pears and refrigerate.
Serves 6

Oranges in Caramel Sauce

8 oranges
1 cup sugar
½ cup cold water
⅔ cup hot water
lace roll-ups to serve

Pare the rind from one orange and finely shred. Cook in boiling water for 1 minute, then drain and dry.

Peel the oranges, removing all the pith. Thinly slice the oranges and hold the slices together with toothpicks. Arrange in individual dishes.

Place the sugar and cold water in a saucepan. Heat gently until dissolved, then boil steadily to a rich brown caramel. Carefully add the hot water and stir until the caramel has melted, heating again if necessary. Let cool.

Pour the caramel over the oranges, sprinkle with the orange rind and refrigerate. Serve with lace roll-ups.
Serves 4

Rich Chocolate Mousse

3 squares (1 oz each)
  semi-sweet
  chocolate
3 eggs, separated
2 tablespoons sherry
TO DECORATE:
sweetened whipped
  cream
chocolate curls (see
  page 65)

Melt the chocolate in a bowl over a pan of hot water, then add the egg yolks and sherry and mix well. Remove from the heat.

Beat the egg whites until fairly stiff, then carefully fold into the chocolate mixture. Divide between four ramekins and place in the refrigerator to set.

Pipe a whipped cream rosette on top of each mousse and sprinkle with chocolate curls.

Serves 4

Orange Mousse

2 envelopes (2
    tablespoons)
    unflavored gelatin
grated rind and juice
    of 1 lemon
1 can (6 oz) frozen
    concentrated
    orange juice,
    thawed
4 eggs
2 egg yolks
½ cup sugar
1½ cups heavy
    cream, whipped
shredded orange rind
    to decorate

Soak the gelatin in the lemon juice.
Place the gelatin mixture and orange
juice in a saucepan and heat, stirring,
until the gelatin dissolves. Cool
slightly.

Beat the eggs, egg yolks, sugar
and lemon rind in a bowl until thick.
Fold in the gelatin mixture with half
the whipped cream. Pour into a
serving bowl and refrigerate until
set.

Decorate with the remaining
whipped cream and the orange rind.
Serves 6 to 8

Strawberry Mousse

1 pint strawberries
2 envelopes (2
  tablespoons)
  unflavored gelatin,
  soaked in ¼ cup
  orange juice
2 eggs
1 egg yolk
½ cup sugar
2 cups heavy cream,
  whipped

Set aside a few strawberries for decoration. Process the remainder in a blender or food processor.

Put the gelatin mixture in a bowl over a pan of simmering water and stir until dissolved. Cool slightly.

Place the eggs, egg yolk and sugar in a bowl and beat until thick. Fold in the gelatin mixture, strawberry purée and three-quarters of the whipped cream. Pour into a 4 cup ring mold. Refrigerate until set.

Invert onto a serving platter. Decorate the mousse with the remaining whipped cream and the reserved strawberries.
Serves 8

Chocolate and Orange Mousse

8 squares (1 oz each)
 semi-sweet
 chocolate
6 tablespoons milk
2 envelopes (2
 tablespoons)
 unflavored gelatin
grated rind and juice
 of 1 orange
4 eggs
2 egg yolks
½ cup sugar
1½ cups heavy
 cream, whipped
chocolate curls to
 decorate (see page
 65)

Place the chocolate and milk in a
small saucepan and heat gently until
melted. Set aside to cool.

Soak the gelatin in the orange juice
for 5 minutes. Place in a bowl over a
pan of simmering water and stir until
the gelatin dissolves. Cool slightly.

Beat the eggs, egg yolks, sugar
and orange rind in a bowl until thick.
Add the gelatin mixture and
chocolate. Stir over a bowl of ice
water until slightly thickened, then
fold in three-quarters of the whipped
cream and spoon into a glass serving
bowl. Refrigerate until set.

Decorate with the remaining
whipped cream and chocolate curls.
Serves 6 to 8

Mousse Brazilienne

2 envelopes (2
  tablespoons)
  unflavored gelatin,
  soaked in ¼ cup
  strong black coffee
3 eggs
2 egg yolks
½ cup sugar
1½ cups heavy
  cream, whipped
½ cup crushed
  praline (see page
  44)
CARAMEL:
½ cup sugar
¼ cup water
¼ cup strong black
  coffee

First make the caramel. Dissolve the
sugar in the water over a low heat,
then cook until a rich brown.
Remove from the heat. Carefully add
the hot coffee, all at once, stirring
until thoroughly blended. Reheat to
melt the caramel if necessary, then
cool.

Place the gelatin mixture in a bowl
over a pan of simmering water and
stir until dissolved. Cool slightly.

Beat the eggs, egg yolks and sugar
in a bowl until thick. Fold in the
gelatin mixture with the whipped
cream and the caramel. Stir gently
over a bowl of ice water until
thickened, then add the praline.

Pour into a greased 8 cup mold
and refrigerate until set.

Invert onto a serving platter and
serve with cream if desired.
Serves 8

Chocolate and Almond Mold

8 squares (1 oz each)
  semi-sweet
  chocolate
5 tablespoons milk
½ cup butter or
  margarine
½ cup sugar
1 can (12 oz)
  almond filling
3 tablespoons brandy
1 cup heavy cream,
  whipped with
  ¼ cup sugar, to
  decorate

Place the chocolate and milk in a
small saucepan and heat gently until
melted, then cool.

Cream the butter and sugar
together until light and fluffy, then
gradually add the almond filling,
beating well between each addition.
Stir in the melted chocolate and
brandy. Pour into a greased 4 cup
mold. Refrigerate overnight.

Invert onto a serving dish and
decorate with piped whipped cream.
Serves 8

Mocha Charlotte

6 squares (1 oz each)
    semi-sweet
    chocolate
2 cups strong black
    coffee
2 eggs, separated
¼ cup sugar
2 envelopes (2
    tablespoons)
    unflavored gelatin,
    soaked in ¼ cup
    cold water
2 cups heavy cream,
    whipped
24 langue de chat
    cookies
grated chocolate to
    decorate

Place the chocolate in a small saucepan with ¾ cup of the coffee. Heat gently until melted, then add the remaining coffee and bring to a boil, stirring. Remove from heat.

Beat the egg yolks and sugar together until creamy. Stir in the coffee mixture. Return to the saucepan and stir over low heat until the custard thickens. Add the gelatin and stir until dissolved. Let cool.

Stir over a bowl of ice water until the mixture starts to thicken, then fold in two-thirds of the whipped cream. Beat the egg whites until stiff and fold into the mixture. Pour into a lightly oiled 1½ quart Charlotte mold and refrigerate until set.

Invert onto a plate. Cover the sides with a thin layer of cream and press on the cookies. Decorate with the remaining cream and chocolate.
Serves 6 to 8

27

Charlotte Russe

6 egg yolks
¾ cup sugar
2 cups milk
1 teaspoon vanilla
2 envelopes (2
    tablespoons)
    unflavored gelatin,
    soaked in ¼ cup
    water
3 cups heavy cream,
    whipped
12 lady fingers, split
glacé cherry and
    angelica pieces to
    decorate

Beat the egg yolks and sugar together until smooth. Bring the milk just to the boiling point. Remove from the heat and stir in the vanilla. Gradually pour over the egg mixture, stirring vigorously with a wire whisk. Pour the mixture into the top of a double boiler and cook over simmering water until thickened. Stir in the gelatin until dissolved. Let cool.

Fold two-thirds of the whipped cream into the custard. Line a 1½ quart Charlotte mold with the lady fingers. Arrange cut pieces of lady fingers in a flower pattern in the bottom of the mold. Pour the custard mixture into the mold and refrigerate until set.

To serve, invert the mold onto a serving platter and pipe the top and bottom edges with the remaining whipped cream. Decorate with the cherry and angelica.

Serves 8

Lime Soufflé

6 eggs, separated
1 cup superfine sugar
grated rind of 1 lime
juice of 3 limes
1 envelope (1
    tablespoon)
    unflavored gelatin,
    soaked in 1/4 cup
    water
green food coloring
    (optional)
1 1/2 cups heavy
    cream, whipped
1/4 teaspoon cream of
    tartar
TO DECORATE:
1/4 cup chopped
    toasted almonds
sweetened whipped
    cream

Tie a collar of doubled waxed paper around a 2 quart soufflé dish to stand 2 inches above the rim. Butter the inside of the paper collar.

Beat the egg yolks and sugar together in a bowl until thick. Add the lime rind and juice and stir well. Pour the mixture into the top of a double boiler and cook over simmering water until thick, stirring occasionally.

Place the gelatin mixture in a bowl over a pan of simmering water and stir until dissolved. Add to the lime mixture with the food coloring, if used, and stir well. Refrigerate until thickened.

Fold the whipped cream into the lime mixture. Beat the egg whites with the cream of tartar until stiff and fold into the lime mixture. Spoon into the soufflé dish and refrigerate until set.

To serve, carefully remove the waxed paper collar and press the almonds around the sides of the soufflé. Decorate the top with piped sweetened whipped cream.
Serves 8 to 10

Lemon Soufflé

3 large eggs,
  separated
¾ cup sugar
grated rind and juice
  of 2 lemons
2 cups heavy cream,
  whipped
2 envelopes (2
  tablespoons)
  unflavored gelatin,
  soaked in 3
  tablespoons water
2 tablespoons
  chopped toasted
  almonds to
  decorate

Tie a collar of doubled waxed paper
around a 6 inch soufflé dish to stand
2 inches above the rim. Butter the
inside of the paper collar.

Place the egg yolks, sugar and
lemon rind in a bowl. Heat the
lemon juice in a small saucepan, then
pour over the egg mixture. Beat
until thick, then fold in two-thirds of
the whipped cream.

Put the gelatin mixture in a bowl
over a pan of simmering water and
stir until dissolved. Add to the lemon
mixture and stir well. Cool until
almost set.

Beat the egg whites until stiff, then
fold into the mixture. Spoon into the
soufflé dish and chill until set.

Carefully remove the paper collar
and press the nuts around the sides.
Spread some of the remaining
cream over the top and pipe the rest
around the edge. Chill before serving.
Serves 6 to 8

Soufflé Omelet

4 eggs, separated
2 tablespoons light
cream
1 tablespoon sugar
1 tablespoon butter or
margarine
3 tablespoons
strawberry jam
confectioners sugar
for sprinkling

Place the egg yolks in a bowl with
the cream and sugar and beat well.
Beat the egg whites until stiff, then
fold into the yolk mixture.

Melt the butter in an 8 inch omelet
pan, then pour in the egg mixture
and spread evenly. Cook over
moderate heat for 2 minutes or until
golden brown underneath.

Put the pan in a preheated 400°F
oven and cook for 3 minutes or until
the top is set.

Heat the jam in a small saucepan.
Heat two skewers until red hot.

Remove the omelet from the oven
and quickly spread with the jam.
Fold over with a narrow spatula and
sprinkle with confectioners sugar.
Slide onto a warm platter and score a
lattice pattern across the top with the
hot skewers. Serve immediately.
Serves 2

Gooseberry Fool

1 can (15¾ oz)
   gooseberries
¼ cup sugar
1 cup heavy cream,
   whipped
few drops of green
   food coloring
langue de chat
   cookies to serve

Place the gooseberries, with their juice, and the sugar in the container of a blender or food processor and process until smooth. Pour into a bowl.

Fold the whipped cream and food coloring into the fruit mixture. Spoon into individual dishes and chill. Serve with langue de chat cookies.

Serves 6

Banana Whip

1 egg white
2 tablespoons sugar
4 ripe bananas,
  mashed
¾ cup heavy cream,
  whipped
vanilla wafers to
  serve

Beat the egg white until stiff, then beat in the sugar. Fold the egg white mixture and mashed bananas into the whipped cream.

Spoon into individual dishes and serve immediately with vanilla wafers.

Serves 4 to 6

Creamy Rice Pudding

1/2 cup rice
2 1/2 cups milk
2 tablespoons sugar
1/4 teaspoon vanilla
3/4 cup heavy cream,
    whipped
APRICOT SAUCE:
2/3 cup dried apricots,
    soaked overnight
    in 2 cups water
1/2 cup sugar
2 teaspoons lemon
    juice

Place the rice and milk in a saucepan and bring to a boil, stirring constantly. Simmer gently for 40 minutes or until tender, adding a little extra milk if necessary. Add the sugar and vanilla and pour into a bowl to cool.

Meanwhile, make the sauce. Simmer the apricots in their soaking water for 15 minutes. Cool slightly, then process in a blender or food processor until smooth. Stir in the sugar and lemon juice.

Fold the whipped cream into the rice. Serve cold with the warm apricot sauce.
Serves 4 to 6

Zabaione

4 egg yolks
1/2 cup sugar
1/4 cup Marsala
lady fingers to serve

Place the egg yolks in a bowl with the sugar and Marsala. Whisk together over a pan of gently simmering water until very thick.

Pour into four glasses and serve immediately with lady fingers.
Serves 4

Prune Whip

1 1/2 cups pitted
    prunes
3/4 cup plain yogurt
2 tablespoons honey
1 1/4 cups heavy
    cream, whipped
2 tablespoons
    chopped walnuts
    to decorate

Place the prunes in a saucepan with just enough water to cover and simmer for 15 minutes or until tender. Drain, reserving 1/2 cup of the cooking liquid. Process the prunes and reserved cooking liquid in a blender or food processor until smooth. Let cool.

Fold the prune purée, yogurt and honey into the whipped cream and spoon into individual glass dishes. Decorate with walnuts.
Serves 6 to 8

Peach Bavarian

2 cups chopped
  peaches
juice of 1 lemon
½ cup sugar
1 envelope (1 table-
  spoon) unflavored
  gelatin, soaked in
  ½ cup water
1½ cups heavy
  cream, whipped
½ teaspoon vanilla
½ teaspoon almond
  extract
TO DECORATE:
whipped cream
peach slices

Mix the peaches, lemon juice and sugar and let stand for 1 hour.

Put the gelatin mixture in a bowl over a pan of simmering water and stir until dissolved. Add to the peach mixture and stir well. Refrigerate until beginning to thicken.

Fold the whipped cream, vanilla and almond extract into the peach mixture. Spoon into six individual ramekins and chill until set.

Decorate with piped whipped cream rosettes and peach slices.
Serves 6

Peach Brûlée

6 fresh peaches,
  peeled
2 tablespoons
  Cointreau
1¼ cups heavy
  cream, whipped
⅔ cup firmly packed
  brown sugar

Cut the peaches in half, remove the pits and place in a shallow ovenproof dish. Pour the Cointreau over.

Spread the cream over the peaches, covering them completely; sprinkle with the sugar. Cook under a hot broiler for 3 minutes.

Cool, then chill before serving.
Serves 6

Sherry Trifle

1 8-inch square
  sponge cake, sliced
3 tablespoons jam
3 egg yolks
2 teaspoons
  cornstarch
2 tablespoons sugar
2 cups milk
5 tablespoons sherry
2 bananas, sliced
¾ cup heavy cream,
  whipped
TO DECORATE:
glacé cherries
sliced toasted almonds

Spread the cake slices with jam and arrange in a glass serving bowl.

Beat the egg yolks with the cornstarch and sugar until smooth. Bring the milk to a boil in a saucepan, pour over the egg yolk mixture and stir well. Pour back into the saucepan and heat gently, stirring constantly, until the mixture is thick enough to coat the back of a wooden spoon. Cool slightly.

Sprinkle the sherry over the sponge cake and top with the bananas. Pour the custard over and let set.

Spread a layer of whipped cream over the top. Decorate with piped whipped cream rosettes, cherries and toasted almonds.

Serves 4

Pots de Chocolat

4 squares (1 oz each)
  semi-sweet
  chocolate
2½ cups milk
2 eggs
2 egg yolks
¼ cup sugar

Place the chocolate and milk in a saucepan and heat gently to melt the chocolate. Beat the eggs, egg yolks and sugar together and stir into the chocolate mixture.

Strain into individual ovenproof china pots or ramekins. Place in a roasting pan containing 1 inch water. Bake in a preheated 350°F oven for 35 to 40 minutes or until just set.

Cool and refrigerate before serving.

Serves 4 to 6

Syllabub

grated rind and juice
  of 1 lemon
½ cup white wine
½ cup sugar
1½ cups heavy
  cream
1 egg white
langue de chat
  cookies to serve

Place the lemon rind and juice in a
bowl with the wine and half the
sugar. Let soak for 1 hour.

Whip the cream until thick, then
gradually add the wine mixture and
continue beating until it holds its
shape.

Beat the egg white until stiff,
then beat in the remaining sugar.
Carefully fold into the whipped
cream mixture. Spoon into four
glasses and serve with langue de chat
cookies.

Serves 4

Crème Caramel

½ cup sugar
3 tablespoons water
3 eggs
2 cups milk
½ teaspoon vanilla

Put 6 tablespoons of the sugar and the water in a saucepan. Heat gently, stirring, until dissolved, then cook to a rich caramel without stirring. Carefully add 1 teaspoon of boiling water and pour into a 1 quart soufflé dish or mold. Let set.

Beat the eggs and remaining sugar together. Heat the milk almost to boiling point and add to the egg mixture with the vanilla. Mix well. Strain into the soufflé dish and place the dish in a roasting pan containing 1 inch of water. Bake in a preheated 275°F oven for 1½ hours or until set. Cool, then invert onto a serving dish.

Serves 4

Apricot Ambrosia

1 can (17 oz) apricot
    halves, drained
1 tablespoon honey
8 coconut macaroons
¾ cup heavy cream,
    whipped
1 tablespoon sliced
    almonds

Place the apricots and honey in a blender or food processor and process until smooth.

Break the macaroons into bite-size pieces. Fold into the whipped cream, together with the apricot purée.

Spoon into four glass dishes and chill. To serve, sprinkle with almonds.

Serves 4

Scottish Delight

⅓ cup chopped
    almonds
½ cup oatmeal
1½ cups heavy
    cream
1 tablespoon lemon
    juice
5 tablespoons scotch
¼ cup honey
lemon twists to
    decorate

Place the almonds and oatmeal under the broiler and brown, turning frequently. Let cool.

Whip the cream until it stands in soft peaks, then beat in the lemon juice, scotch and honey.

Fold in the almonds and oatmeal. Spoon into six glasses and refrigerate. Decorate with lemon twists before serving.

Serves 6

St Clement's Ice Cream

3 eggs, separated
¾ cup sugar
grated rind and juice
  of 1 lemon
grated rind and juice
  of 1 orange
1½ cups heavy
  cream, whipped

Beat the egg yolks, half the sugar and the lemon and orange rinds together until thick and creamy. Pour the fruit juices into a saucepan and heat gently, then pour over the egg mixture and continue beating until thick.

Beat the egg whites until stiff, then beat in the remaining sugar. Fold into the fruit mixture with the whipped cream.

Spoon into a freezerproof container. Cover, seal and freeze until firm.

Spoon into chilled glasses and serve.

Serves 6 to 8

Iced Mocha Mousse

3 eggs, separated
1/2 cup sugar
2 squares (1 oz each)
  semi-sweet
  chocolate
1 tablespoon instant
  coffee
2 tablespoons water
3/4 cup heavy cream,
  whipped
chocolate curls to
  decorate

Beat the egg yolks with the sugar until thick and creamy.

Place the chocolate, coffee and water in the top of a double boiler and heat gently until melted, then beat into the egg mixture. Fold in the whipped cream.

Beat the egg whites until stiff and carefully fold into the chocolate mixture. Pour into individual ramekins. Cover and freeze for 3 to 4 hours.

Place in the refrigerator 10 minutes before serving to soften. Decorate with chocolate curls.
Serves 4 to 6

Vanilla Ice Cream

2 eggs
2 egg yolks
⅓ cup sugar
2 cups milk or
  half and half
⅛ teaspoon vanilla
1½ cups heavy
  cream, whipped
langue de chat or
  gaufrettes cookies
  to serve

Mix the eggs, egg yolks and sugar together. Bring the milk gently to a boil and pour over the egg mixture, stirring vigorously. Stir in the vanilla. Let cool, then fold in the whipped cream.

Pour into a freezerproof container. Cover and freeze for 1 hour. Remove and stir well, then freeze until firm.

Place in the refrigerator 20 minutes before serving to soften. Spoon into chilled glasses and serve with cookies.

Serves 8

VARIATIONS:

Chocolate: Melt 8 squares (1 oz each) semi-sweet chocolate with the milk.

Praline: Place ½ cup blanched almonds and ¼ cup sugar in a saucepan and heat gently until the sugar melts. Cook, stirring, until nut brown. Pour onto a greased cookie sheet and let set. Crush with a rolling pin and add with the whipped cream.

Coffee: Dissolve 3 tablespoons instant coffee in 2 tablespoons boiling water, cool and add with the whipped cream.

Ginger: Add ½ cup finely chopped preserved ginger to the eggs and sugar. Add 2 tablespoons of the ginger syrup with the whipped cream.

Banana Ice

1 can (13 oz)
 evaporated milk,
 chilled
⅔ cup firmly packed
 brown sugar
3 ripe bananas
1 tablespoon lemon
 juice
vanilla wafers to
 serve

Beat the evaporated milk until very thick, then beat in the sugar. Mash the bananas with the lemon juice, then beat into the evaporated milk.

Pour into a freezerproof container. Cover and freeze for 1 hour. Stir well, then freeze until firm.

Place in the refrigerator 30 minutes before serving to soften. Spoon into chilled glasses and serve with vanilla wafers.
Serves 6 to 8

45

Strawberry Ice Cream

1 pint strawberries
2 envelopes (2
 tablespoons)
 unflavored gelatin,
 soaked in ¼ cup
 cold water
1 can (13 oz)
 evaporated milk,
 chilled
¾ cup sugar
juice of ½ lemon
8 strawberries to
 decorate

Process the strawberries in a blender or food processor until smooth. Strain to remove the pits.

Place the gelatin mixture in a bowl over a pan of simmering water and stir until dissolved. Add to the strawberry purée.

Beat the evaporated milk until thick, then add the sugar, strawberry purée and lemon juice. Pour into a freezerproof container. Cover and freeze for 1 hour. Remove from the freezer and stir well, then freeze until firm.

Place in the refrigerator 20 minutes before serving to soften. Spoon into chilled glasses and decorate each with a strawberry.
Serves 8

Pineapple Ice Cream

1 large pineapple
3 egg whites
¾ cup sugar
1½ cups heavy
 cream, whipped

Cut the pineapple in half lengthwise. Scoop out the flesh and juice into a bowl, discarding the core. Finely chop the flesh. Chill the shells.

Beat the egg whites until stiff, then gradually beat in the sugar. Fold in the whipped cream and pineapple.

Place in a freezerproof container. Cover and freeze for 1 hour. Remove from the freezer and stir well, then freeze until firm.

Place in the refrigerator 20 minutes before serving to soften. Spoon into the chilled pineapple shells and arrange on a serving dish or spoon into chilled glass dishes to serve.
Serves 6 to 8

Bombe Noël

1/3 cup chopped glacé
  cherries
1/3 cup chopped
  angelica
1/3 cup chopped glacé
  pineapple
1/3 cup chopped
  crystallized ginger
1/3 cup raisins
2 tablespoons brandy
2 tablespoons
  Cointreau
3 egg yolks
1/2 cup sugar
1 1/2 cups half and
  half
1/8 teaspoon vanilla
1 1/2 cups heavy
  cream, whipped
TO DECORATE:
angelica and glacé
  pineapple

Put the cherries, angelica, pineapple,
ginger and raisins in a bowl. Pour
the brandy and Cointreau over and
let soak for 1 hour.

Beat the egg yolks and sugar
together until creamy. Bring the half
and half slowly to a boil, then pour
over the egg mixture, stirring
vigorously. Add the vanilla and let
cool.

Fold half the whipped cream and
the fruit into the custard. Place in a
freezerproof container. Cover and
freeze for 1 hour. Remove from
the freezer and stir well. Pour into a
1 1/2 quart ice cream mold, cover with
foil and freeze until firm.

Dip the mold into cold water and
invert the bombe onto a chilled
serving plate. Pipe the remaining
whipped cream in rosettes around
the bombe and decorate with
angelica and glacé pineapple.
Serves 6 to 8

Biscuit Tortoni

½ cup ground
  almonds
1 cup amaretti biscuit
  crumbs
1½ cups light cream
1 teaspoon vanilla
½ cup sugar
3 tablespoons rum or
  cream sherry
2 cups heavy cream,
  whipped
amaretti crumbs to
  decorate

Mix the ground almonds and
amaretti crumbs in a bowl. Combine
the light cream and vanilla, pour
over the crumbs and let soak for 30
minutes. Stir in the sugar and rum
and spoon into a freezerproof
container. Freeze until ice crystals
form around the sides.

Fold the whipped cream into the
almond mixture. Spoon into
individual freezerproof dishes and
cover with plastic wrap. Freeze until
firm.

Place in the refrigerator 10 minutes
before serving to soften. Sprinkle
with amaretti crumbs.
Serves 6 to 8

Blackberry Ice Cream

1 pint blackberries
6 tablespoons sugar
½ cup water
3 egg yolks
2 cups light cream
2 tablespoons
   confectioners sugar
gaufrette cookies to
   serve

Put the blackberries in a saucepan with 2 tablespoons of the sugar and simmer for 10 minutes or until tender. Press through a mesh strainer and let the purée cool.

Put the water and remaining sugar in a saucepan and heat gently, stirring, until sugar has dissolved. Increase the heat and boil steadily until the syrup reaches the soft ball stage. Test with a candy thermometer – it should register 230°F.

Cool the syrup slightly, then pour over the egg yolks, beating until the mixture is thick.

Mix the cream with the blackberry purée and confectioners sugar and fold into the beaten egg mixture.

Pour into a freezerproof container. Cover and freeze until firm.

Place in the refrigerator 20 minutes before serving to soften. Spoon into chilled glasses and serve with gaufrette cookies.
Serves 8

Pineapple Ice Cream Meringue

MERINGUE:
4 egg whites
1 cup sugar
FILLING:
1/2 recipe Pineapple
  Ice Cream (see
  page 46)
1 1/2 cups heavy
  cream
1/4 cup thinly sliced
  preserved ginger
2 tablespoons ginger
  syrup
TO DECORATE:
sweetened whipped
  cream
sliced preserved
  ginger

Make the meringue, pipe and cook three 6 inch rounds as for Chestnut Vacherin (see page 84).

Remove the pineapple ice cream from the freezer and allow to thaw for 10 minutes at room temperature.

Whip the cream until it forms soft peaks. Fold in the ginger and syrup.

Spread a thin layer of pineapple ice cream in the bottom of an 8 inch springform pan. Place a meringue round on top and cover with half the whipped cream. Repeat these layers and top with the third meringue round, filling the space at the sides with pineapple ice cream. Cover with foil and freeze for 3 to 4 hours.

Place in the refrigerator 20 minutes before serving to soften. Invert onto a serving platter and decorate with piped whipped cream and ginger.
Serves 8

Bombe au Chocolat

CHOCOLATE ICE
  CREAM:
2 eggs
2 egg yolks
⅓ cup sugar
*2 cups milk or half
  and half*
*8 squares (1 oz each)
  semi-sweet
  chocolate*
*1½ cups heavy
  cream, whipped*
FILLING:
1 tablespoon rum
*1 tablespoon
  confectioners sugar*
3 bananas, sliced
*¾ cup heavy cream,
  whipped*

Make the chocolate ice cream (see
page 44) and freeze until almost firm.

To make the filling, fold the rum,
confectioners sugar and bananas into
the whipped cream.

Line the sides of a chilled 1½ quart
bombe mold thickly with the
chocolate ice cream. Fill the center
with the banana filling and cover
with any remaining chocolate ice
cream. Cover the bombe with a lid
or aluminum foil and freeze for 4
hours.

Dip the mold into cold water and
invert the bombe onto a chilled
serving platter.
Serves 6 to 8

51

Mint Sherbet

2 cups water
1/2 cup sugar
thinly pared rind and
    juice of 2 lemons
1/4 cup mint leaves
few drops of green
    food coloring
1 egg white
TO DECORATE:
small mint leaves
sugar for sprinkling

Put the water, sugar and lemon rind and juice in a saucepan and heat gently, stirring, until the sugar has dissolved. Bring to a boil and simmer for 5 minutes, then add the mint leaves, cover and let cool. Strain and add the food coloring. Pour into a freezerproof container. Cover and freeze.

When partially frozen, beat most of the egg white until stiff and fold into the mint ice. Cover and freeze until firm.

Brush the small mint leaves with the reserved egg white. Sprinkle with sugar and leave to dry for about 1 hour.

Place the sherbet in the refrigerator 10 minutes before serving to soften. Spoon into chilled glasses and decorate with sugared mint leaves.
Serves 6

Raspberry Ice

1 pint raspberries
1/2 cup sugar
2/3 cup water
juice of 1/2 lemon
1 egg white

Process the raspberries in a blender or food processor until smooth. Strain to remove the pits.

Place the sugar and water in a saucepan and heat gently, stirring until dissolved. Bring to a boil and simmer for 5 minutes; let cool. Add to the raspberry purée with the lemon juice. Pour into a freezerproof container. Cover and freeze.

When partially frozen, beat the egg white until stiff and fold into the raspberry ice. Freeze until firm. Place in the refrigerator 10 minutes before serving to soften.
Serves 4

Orange Sherbet

2 cups water
½ cup sugar
thinly pared rind and
    juice of 1 lemon
1 can (6 oz) frozen
    concentrated
    orange juice,
    thawed
1 egg white

Place the water, sugar and lemon rind and juice in a saucepan and heat gently, stirring until dissolved. Bring to a boil, simmer for 5 minutes, then let cool.

Remove the lemon rind and stir in the orange juice. Pour into a freezerproof container. Cover and freeze.

When partially frozen, beat the egg white until stiff and fold into the orange ice. Freeze until firm, stirring once or twice during freezing.

Place in the refrigerator 10 minutes before serving to soften. Spoon into chilled glasses.

Serves 6

53

Raspberry Fluff

1 pint raspberries
2 egg whites
½ cup sugar
1½ cups heavy
  cream, whipped
1 tablespoon
  Cointreau
vanilla wafers to
  serve

Process the raspberries in a blender or food processor until smooth. Strain to remove the pits. Place in a freezerproof container. Cover and freeze for 1 to 2 hours or until partially frozen.

Beat the egg whites until stiff. Beat in the sugar, a tablespoon at a time; the mixture should be very stiff.

Beat the raspberry purée with a fork. Fold the whipped cream into the egg white mixture, then carefully fold in the raspberry purée and the Cointreau.

Spoon into chilled glasses and serve immediately with vanilla wafers.

Serves 4 to 6

Bombe Grand Marnier

2½ cups heavy
  cream
1 tablespoon
  confectioners sugar
¼ lb bought or
  homemade
  meringues
2 tablespoons Grand
  Marnier
TO DECORATE:
¾ cup heavy cream,
  whipped
shredded orange rind

Whip the cream until soft peaks form. Add the confectioners sugar and continue whipping until stiff. Break the meringues into pieces and fold into the whipped cream with the Grand Marnier. Spoon into a 5 cup metal bowl, cover with foil and freeze until firm.

Invert onto a serving dish 30 minutes before serving. Decorate with piped whipped cream and orange rind.

Serves 8

Avocado Ice Cream

2 ripe avocados,
  peeled and pitted
¾ cup light cream or
  half and half
1¼ cups heavy
  cream, whipped
½ cup sugar
juice of ½ lemon
½ cup chopped
  toasted almonds
vanilla wafers to
  serve

Process the avocados and light cream in a blender or food processor until smooth.

Fold the avocado mixture into the whipped cream with the sugar, lemon juice and toasted almonds. Place in a freezerproof container. Cover and freeze until firm.

Place in the refrigerator 20 minutes before serving to soften. Spoon into four chilled glasses and serve with vanilla wafers.

Serves 4

Honey Lemon Tart

BASIC PIE CRUST:
*1¾ cups all-purpose
    flour*
½ teaspoon salt
*½ cup butter or
    margarine*
*3-4 tablespoons ice
    water*

FILLING:
¾ cup corn syrup
½ cup honey
*2 cups soft white
    bread crumbs*
1 egg, beaten
*grated rind of 1
    lemon*

Sift the flour and salt into a bowl. Cut in the butter until the mixture resembles coarse crumbs. Add the water, a tablespoon at a time, and mix to form a firm dough. Gather into a ball.

Roll out two-thirds of the dough into an 11 inch round. Use to line a 9 inch flan or quiche pan. Chill the shell and remaining dough for 15 minutes.

Combine the corn syrup, honey, bread crumbs, egg and lemon rind and pour into the shell. Roll out the remaining dough and cut into long narrow strips. Use to make a twisted lattice pattern over the filling.

Bake in a preheated 400°F oven for 25 to 30 minutes or until the filling is set. Serve warm with cream.
Serves 8 to 10

Lemon Meringue Pie

1 recipe basic pie
  crust (see opposite
  page)
½ cup cornstarch
1¼ cups water
2 tablespoons butter
  or margarine
grated rind and juice
  of 2 lemons
2 eggs, separated
¾ cup sugar

Roll out the dough and use to line an 8 inch pie plate. Line with aluminum foil and dried beans and bake in a preheated 400°F oven for 15 to 20 minutes. Remove the foil and beans and return to the oven to bake for 5 minutes longer. Cool on a wire rack.

Blend the cornstarch with a little of the water in a small saucepan. Add the remaining water and the butter. Bring to a boil slowly, stirring constantly. Simmer, stirring, for 3 minutes. Remove from the heat and add the lemon rind and juice, egg yolks and ¼ cup sugar. Pour into the baked pie shell.

Beat the egg whites until very stiff, then beat in the remaining sugar and spread over the lemon filling.

Bake in a preheated 400°F oven for 8 to 10 minutes or until lightly browned. Serve cold.
Serves 6 to 8

Deep-Dish Apple Pie

1½ lb tart apples,
  peeled, cored and
  thinly sliced
½ cup firmly packed
  brown sugar
1 teaspoon ground
  cinnamon
½ teaspoon grated
  nutmeg
¼ teaspoon ground
  cloves
½ recipe basic pie
  crust (see page 56)
water and sugar to
  glaze

Layer the apples with the sugar and
spices in a 9 inch deep dish pie plate,
finishing with a layer of apples.

Roll out the dough to a round
about 2 inches larger than the pie
plate. Cut off a narrow strip all
around and use to cover the rim of
the pie plate; brush with water.

Lift the dough round on the
rolling pin and place over the apples,
sealing the edges well. Trim and
flute the edges; make a vent in the
center.

Brush with water, sprinkle with
sugar and bake in a preheated 400°F
oven for 30 to 40 minutes.

Serve warm or cold, with whipped
cream if desired.

Serves 4 to 6

VARIATION:

**Deep-dish apple and blueberry
pie:** Use 1 lb tart apples and ½ pint
blueberries. Omit the cinnamon and
the ground cloves. Proceed as
directed above, layering the
blueberries with the apple slices and
nutmeg. Serve warm or cold, with
whipped cream if desired.

French Apple Tart

PÂTE SUCRÉE:
1½ cups all-purpose
   flour
6 tablespoons butter
⅓ cup sugar
3 egg yolks
⅛ teaspoon vanilla
FILLING:
3 lb tart apples,
   peeled, cored and
   thinly sliced
¼ cup sugar
GLAZE:
¼ cup apricot jam
juice of ½ lemon

Sift the flour onto a marble slab or cold work surface. Make a well in the center and add the butter, sugar, egg yolks and vanilla. Using your fingertips work these ingredients together, drawing in the flour. Knead until smooth and chill for 1 hour.

Roll out the dough very thinly and use to line a 10 inch flan or quiche pan. Fill with the apples, arranging an overlapping layer of apples on top. Sprinkle with the sugar.

Bake in a preheated 375°F oven for 35 to 40 minutes or until the pastry is golden and the apples are just tender.

Meanwhile, heat the jam with the lemon juice, strain, and brush over the apples. Serve hot or cold, with cream, if desired.
Serves 8

Mince Pies

RICH PASTRY:
2 cups all-purpose
  flour
1/2 teaspoon salt
5 tablespoons butter
  or margarine
5 tablespoons
  shortening
1 tablespoon sugar
1 egg yolk
3-4 tablespoons ice
  water
milk to glaze
confectioners sugar
  for sprinkling
FILLING:
6 tablespoons
  mincemeat
2 tablespoons brandy

Sift the flour and salt into a bowl and cut in the butter and shortening until the mixture resembles coarse crumbs. Stir in the sugar and egg yolk. Add the ice water, a tablespoon at a time, and toss with a fork. Gather into a ball and knead lightly. Chill for 15 minutes.

Roll out half the dough very thinly on a floured surface and cut out 12 rounds using a 3 inch fluted cutter. Use to line a 12 cup muffin pan. Roll out the remaining dough and cut into 12 rounds using a 2½ inch fluted cutter.

Combine the mincemeat and brandy and spoon a little into each pastry shell. Place the smaller rounds on top of the filling and press the edges together. Make a hole in the center of each and brush the tops with milk.

Bake in a preheated 400°F oven for 15 to 20 minutes or until golden. Sprinkle with confectioners sugar and serve warm.
Makes 12

Mincemeat Tart

1 recipe rich pastry
    (see opposite page)
water and sugar to
    glaze
FILLING:
1 jar (16 oz)
    mincemeat
2 apples, peeled,
    cored and chopped
1/4 lb seedless grapes,
    halved
grated rind of 1
    orange
2 tablespoons brandy
TO SERVE:
2 tablespoons brandy
3/4 cup heavy cream,
    whipped with
    1/4 cup sugar

Roll out two-thirds of the dough and
use to line a 9 inch flan or quiche
pan. Chill the shell and remaining
dough for 15 minutes.
　　Mix the filling ingredients
together and fill the shell.
　　Roll out the remaining dough and
cut out 12 rounds using a 3 inch
fluted cutter. Dampen the edges of
the pastry shell and arrange the
rounds overlapping around the edge.
　　Brush with water, sprinkle with
sugar and bake in a preheated 400°F
oven for 35 to 40 minutes or until
golden.
　　Fold the brandy into the whipped
cream. Serve the tart hot or cold
with the whipped cream.
Serves 6 to 8

Blueberry Pie

PASTRY:
1¾ cups all-purpose
   flour
½ teaspoon salt
½ cup butter or
   margarine
3-4 tablespoons ice
   water

FILLING:
1 pint blueberries
¼ cup water
½ cup firmly packed
   brown sugar
1 tablespoon
   cornstarch
½ teaspoon ground
   cinnamon
2 teaspoons grated
   lemon rind
1 tablespoon lemon
   juice
sugar for sprinkling

Sift the flour and salt into a bowl.
Cut in the butter until the mixture
resembles coarse crumbs. Add the
water, a tablespoon at a time, and
toss with a fork. Gather into a ball
and knead lightly.

Roll out two-thirds of the dough
into a 11 inch round. Use to line a
9 inch flan or quiche pan. Chill the
shell and remaining dough for 15
minutes.

Place the blueberries, water and
sugar in a saucepan, cover and cook
for 10 minutes. Add the cornstarch,
cinnamon and lemon rind and juice
and stir well. Cook until the mixture
thickens. Let cool.

Spoon the blueberry mixture into
the pastry shell. Roll out the
remaining dough and cut into long
narrow strips. Use to make a lattice
pattern over the filling. Brush with
water and sprinkle with sugar.

Bake in a preheated 400°F oven for
25 to 30 minutes or until the crust is
golden. Serve warm or cold.
Serves 8 to 10

Fruit Tart

1 sheet (½ of a
  17¼ oz pkg)
  frozen puff pastry,
  thawed
1 egg yolk, mixed
  with 1 teaspoon
  water
GLAZE:
¼ cup apricot jam
2 tablespoons water
1 teaspoon lemon
  juice
FILLING:
¼ lb black grapes,
  pitted
¼ lb seedless grapes
½ pint strawberries

Roll out the dough to a 12 × 8 inch
rectangle. Sprinkle the dough lightly
with flour and fold in half
lengthwise.

Cut out a rectangle from the
folded edge, leaving a 1½ inch wide
band on the remaining three sides.

Open out the rectangle and roll
out to 12 × 8 inches. Place on a
dampened cookie sheet, prick all
over and dampen the edges.

Open out the band of dough and
place on the rectangle to make a
border. Flute the edges and score a
pattern on the border with a knife.
Brush the border with the egg yolk
mixture and bake in a preheated
425°F oven for 20 to 25 minutes or
until golden brown.

Heat the jam with the water and
lemon juice, strain and reheat. Brush
over the bottom of the pastry case,
then arrange the fruit in rows on top.
Generously brush with the glaze.
Serve cold.
Serves 6

Raisin Cheesecake

*6 tablespoons butter
  or margarine*
½ cup sugar
*grated rind and juice
  of 1 lemon*
*1½ cups
  creamy-style
  cottage cheese*
2 eggs, separated
*½ cup ground
  almonds*
*¼ cup all-purpose
  flour, sifted*
½ cup golden raisins
*confectioners sugar
  for sprinkling*

Cream the butter, sugar and lemon rind together until light and fluffy. Beat in the cottage cheese gradually, then add the egg yolks and beat thoroughly. Add the almonds, flour, raisins and lemon juice and mix well. Beat the egg whites until stiff and carefully fold into the cheese mixture.

Spoon into a greased 8 inch loose-bottomed cake pan and bake in a preheated 350°F oven for 50 to 60 minutes. Turn off the heat and leave the cheesecake in the oven until cooled.

Remove from the pan and sprinkle with confectioners sugar.
Serves 6 to 8

Chocolate Cheesecake

4 tablespoons butter
  or margarine,
  melted
2 cups graham
  cracker crumbs
1/3 cup firmly packed
  brown sugar
6 squares (1 oz each)
  semi-sweet
  chocolate
1 pkg (8 oz) cream
  cheese, softened
1/2 cup granulated
  sugar
2 eggs, separated
1 1/2 cups heavy
  cream, whipped
chocolate curls to
  decorate (see note)

Combine the melted butter, graham cracker crumbs and brown sugar. Press the mixture over the bottom and sides of a 9 inch quiche pan. Place in the refrigerator and leave until set.

Melt the chocolate in a bowl over a pan of hot water. Combine the cream cheese, granulated sugar and egg yolks, then stir in the chocolate. Fold in half the whipped cream.

Beat the egg whites until stiff and fold into the mixture. Pour into the crumb crust and place in the refrigerator to set.

Whip the remaining cream until stiff. Decorate the cheesecake with piped whipped cream and chocolate curls.

Serves 6

NOTE: To make chocolate curls, shave thin layers from a block of chocolate, using a potato peeler.

PUDDINGS

Raisin Bread Pudding

6 slices raisin bread,
    crusts removed
½ teaspoon ground
    cinnamon
¼ teaspoon grated
    nutmeg
4 eggs
½ cup sugar
2½ cups milk

Cut each slice of bread into quarters. Arrange half the pieces in the bottom of a greased 1½ quart casserole. Sprinkle with half the spices and top with the remaining bread pieces and spices.

Beat the eggs and sugar together until smooth. Add the milk and beat until well blended. Pour over the bread and let stand for 1 hour.

Place the casserole in a roasting pan containing 1 inch of water. Bake in a preheated 350°F oven for 55 to 65 minutes or until a knife inserted in the center comes out clean.

Serve warm with heavy cream, if desired.

Serves 6 to 8

Indian Pudding

3½ cups milk
½ cup cornmeal
¼ cup firmly packed
  brown sugar
¼ cup granulated
  sugar
¼ cup molasses
½ teaspoon salt
4 tablespoons butter
  or margarine
½ teaspoon ground
  cinnamon
¼ teaspoon grated
  nutmeg
chopped toasted
  almonds to
  decorate

Heat 2 cups of the milk in a saucepan until very hot. Pour over the cornmeal, stirring constantly. Stir in the remaining milk and cook over low heat for 20 minutes, stirring occasionally.

Add the sugars, molasses, salt, butter, cinnamon and nutmeg and stir well. Spoon into a buttered 2½ pint soufflé dish or casserole. Bake in a preheated 325°F oven for 1½ to 2 hours or until set.

Sprinkle with the toasted almonds and serve warm with vanilla ice cream or heavy cream.

Serves 6 to 8

Lemon Pudding

4 tablespoons butter
  or margarine
grated rind and juice
  of 1 large lemon
½ cup sugar
2 eggs, separated
¼ cup all-purpose
  flour
¾ cup milk

Cream the butter with the lemon rind and sugar until light and fluffy. Mix in the egg yolks, flour and lemon juice, then gradually stir in the milk. Beat the egg whites until stiff and carefully fold into the mixture.

Pour into a greased 1 quart baking dish and place in a roasting pan containing 1 inch water.

Bake in a preheated 350°F oven for 40 to 45 minutes or until set and golden brown. Serve warm.
Serves 4

Rhubarb and Apple Crumble

6 tablespoons butter
  or margarine
1¾ cups whole
  wheat flour
½ cup firmly packed
  brown sugar
1 lb apples, peeled,
  cored and sliced
½ lb rhubarb, cut
  into 1 inch pieces
½ cup granulated
  sugar

Cut the butter into the flour until the mixture resembles coarse crumbs, then stir in the brown sugar. Set the crumble mixture aside.

Layer the apples, rhubarb and granulated sugar in a 1 quart baking dish.

Sprinkle the crumble mixture over the fruit to cover completely. Bake in a preheated 350°F oven for 40 to 50 minutes or until crisp and golden brown.

Serve hot or cold with cream or custard sauce.
Serves 4 to 6

Bread and Butter Pudding

6 slices white bread,
crusts removed
4 tablespoons butter
or margarine
1/3 cup raisins
1/4 cup sugar
2 large eggs
2 1/2 cups milk
grated nutmeg

Spread the bread with the butter and cut each slice into quarters. Arrange half the bread pieces in a 1 1/2 quart baking dish, buttered side down. Sprinkle with the raisins and half the sugar. Cover with the remaining bread pieces, buttered side up.

Beat the eggs and milk together and pour over the bread. Sprinkle with the remaining sugar and nutmeg and let stand for 30 minutes.

Bake in a preheated 325°F oven for 50 to 60 minutes or until the top is golden. Serve with cream.
Serves 4

Apple Pudding

1 lb apples, peeled,
    cored and thinly
    sliced
⅓ cup firmly packed
    brown sugar
½ cup butter or
    margarine
½ cup granulated
    sugar
2 eggs
1 cup self-rising
    flour, sifted
1 tablespoon hot
    water

Put the apples in a greased 1½ quart casserole and sprinkle with the brown sugar.

Cream the butter with the granulated sugar until light and fluffy. Add the eggs, one at a time, adding a little flour with the second egg. Fold in the remaining flour, then stir in the hot water.

Spread the batter evenly over the apples and bake in a preheated 350°F oven for 40 to 45 minutes or until golden brown.

Serve warm or cold with cream if desired.

Serves 4

Steamed Chocolate Pudding

PUDDING:
1⅓ cups self-rising
  flour
⅓ cup cocoa
½ cup butter or
  margarine
1 cup sugar
2 eggs
¼ cup milk

CHOCOLATE SAUCE:
½ cup semi-sweet
  chocolate pieces
¼ cup light corn
  syrup
2 tablespoons butter
  or margarine
2 tablespoons water
½ teaspoon vanilla

Sift the flour and cocoa together.
Cream the butter and sugar until
light and fluffy. Beat in the eggs, one
at a time, adding a little flour with
the second egg. Fold in the
remaining flour mixture, then add
the milk and stir well.

Spoon the batter into a greased
1½ quart bowl. Cover with greased
aluminum foil. Steam for 1½ to
1¾ hours.

To make the sauce, melt the
chocolate with the corn syrup and
butter in the top of a double boiler.
Add the water and vanilla and stir
well.

Invert the pudding onto a warmed
serving platter and pour the warm
sauce over the pudding.
Serves 6 to 8

Apricot Upside-Down Cake

1 cup butter or margarine
⅓ cup firmly packed brown sugar
1 can (16 oz) apricot halves, or cooked fresh apricots, halved and pitted
¾ cup granulated sugar
3 eggs
1½ cups self-rising flour, sifted
1 teaspoon ground allspice

Melt 4 tablespoons of the butter, mix with the brown sugar and spread over the bottom of a 1½ quart baking dish. Drain the apricots, reserving 3 tablespoons of the juice. Arrange the apricot halves, cut side down, in the baking dish.

Cream the remaining butter with the granulated sugar until light and fluffy. Add the eggs, one at a time, adding a little of the flour with the last two eggs. Fold in the remaining flour, the allspice and reserved apricot juice.

Spread the batter over the apricots and bake in a preheated 350°F oven for 55 to 60 minutes or until the sponge springs back when lightly pressed.

Invert onto a warmed serving platter and serve with cream.
Serves 6

Crisp Apple Bake

10 slices white bread,
   crusts removed
6 tablespoons butter
   or margarine
1½-2 lb apples,
   peeled, cored and
   sliced
½ cup firmly packed
   brown sugar

Spread the bread with the butter and cut each slice into quarters. Butter a 1½ quart baking dish generously and line with some of the bread pieces, buttered side down.

Cover with half the apples, sprinkle with sugar and arrange another layer of bread over the top. Cover with the remaining apples, sprinkle with sugar and top with the remaining bread, buttered side up and slightly overlapping. Sprinkle with the remaining sugar.

Cover with foil and bake in a preheated 350°F oven for 35 minutes. Remove the foil and bake for a further 5 minutes or until crisp and golden. Serve hot with cream or vanilla ice cream, if desired.
Serves 6

Blackberry and Apple Layers

½ cup butter or
    margarine
1 lb apples, peeled,
    cored and sliced
½ pint blackberries
½ cup firmly packed
    brown sugar
2 cups soft bread
    crumbs

Melt 2 tablespoons of the butter in a saucepan. Add the apples, blackberries and 3 tablespoons of the sugar. Cover and simmer gently until tender.

Melt the remaining butter in a skillet, add the bread crumbs and sauté until golden brown. Cool, then stir in the remaining sugar.

Divide half the fruit between four individual glass dishes and cover with half the crumbs. Repeat the layers.

Serve chilled with whipped cream.
Serves 4

Christmas Pudding

1½ cups all-purpose
    flour
2 teaspoons ground
    allspice
1 teaspoon ground
    cinnamon
½ teaspoon grated
    nutmeg
3 cups soft white
    bread crumbs
¾ cup butter or
    margarine
1 cup firmly packed
    brown sugar
2 cups golden raisins
1⅓ cups dark raisins
1⅓ cups currants
½ cup diced mixed
    candied fruit peel
grated rind and juice
    of 1 orange
2 eggs, beaten
½ cup dark beer

Sift the flour and spices into a bowl, add the bread crumbs, then cut in the butter. Stir in the sugar, add the remaining ingredients and mix thoroughly.

Pour into a greased 1½ quart ovenproof mixing bowl, cover with waxed paper and foil, and steam for 6 hours, adding more boiling water as necessary.

Cool slightly, then remove the paper and foil and cool completely. Cover with fresh waxed paper and foil and store in a cool dry place.

To serve, steam the pudding again for 2 to 2½ hours. Invert onto a warmed serving plate. If desired, pour over 2 to 3 tablespoons warmed brandy and ignite. Top with a sprig of holly and serve with cream or Brandy Butter.
Serves 8 to 10
NOTE: Christmas Pudding improves with keeping as it allows the mixture to mature. If possible, make it 3 to 4 months before Christmas.

Brandy Butter

¾ cup unsalted
   butter
¾ cup sugar
3-4 tablespoons
   brandy

Cream the butter until soft, then
gradually add the sugar and brandy,
beating thoroughly after each
addition.

    Spoon into a serving dish. Chill
until firm.

Serves 8 to 10

Malakoff Gâteau

6 tablespoons butter
½ cup sugar
1 egg yolk
1 cup ground
  almonds
½ cup light cream
3 tablespoons brandy
1¼ cups strong black
  coffee
24 lady fingers
¾ cup heavy cream
sliced blanched
  almonds to
  decorate

Cream the butter and sugar together until light and fluffy. Add the egg yolk, almonds and light cream and beat until smooth.

Add the brandy to the coffee and quickly dip the lady fingers into it. Arrange some in the bottom of a greased 8 × 4 inch loaf pan.

Spread half the almond mixture on top. Repeat the layers once more, then finish with a layer of lady fingers. Chill until set.

Invert onto a serving platter. Spread two-thirds of the whipped cream over the gâteau. Pipe the remaining cream on top and sprinkle with almonds.

Serves 6 to 8

Zucotto

1 recipe chocolate
   sponge mixture
1/4 cup brandy
2 cups heavy cream
1/3 cup confectioners
   sugar
2 squares (1 oz each)
   semi-sweet
   chocolate, chopped
1/4 cup chopped
   toasted almonds
1/2 lb dark sweet
   cherries, pitted
2 tablespoons Kirsch
1 tablespoon
   unsweetened cocoa

Prepare the sponge mixture as for
Black Forest Gâteau (see page 86).
Pour into a greased 8 inch cake pan.
Bake in a preheated 350°F oven for
35 to 40 minutes. Invert onto a wire
rack to cool.

Split the sponge into two layers
and line a 1½ quart mixing bowl
with one layer, shaping it to fit.
Sprinkle with the brandy and set
aside.

Whip the cream until it forms soft
peaks. Fold in ¼ cup confectioners
sugar, the chocolate, almonds,
cherries and Kirsch. Spoon into the
cake-lined bowl and top with the
remaining sponge. Cover with a
plate and chill for 2 to 3 hours.

Invert onto a serving plate and
sprinkle with the remaining
confectioners sugar and cocoa in
a pattern.
Serves 6 to 8

Crêpes Suzette

BATTER:
1 cup all-purpose
  flour
pinch of salt
1 egg, beaten
1½ cups milk
1 tablespoon oil
ORANGE SAUCE:
4 tablespoons butter
  or margarine
¼ cup sugar
grated rind and juice
  of 2 oranges
2 tablespoons Grand
  Marnier
2 tablespoons brandy

Sift the flour and salt into a bowl and make a well in the center. Add the egg, then gradually add half the milk, stirring constantly. Add the oil and beat thoroughly until smooth. Add the remaining milk and let stand for 30 minutes.

Heat a 6 inch crêpe pan and add a few drops of oil. Pour in 1 tablespoon of batter and tilt the pan to coat the bottom evenly. Cook until the underside is brown, then turn over and cook for 10 seconds. Slide the crêpe out of the pan. Repeat with the remaining batter, stacking the cooked crêpes, one on top of the other.

To make the orange sauce, melt the butter in a skillet, add the sugar and orange rind and juice and heat until bubbling. Dip each crêpe into the sauce, fold into quarters and place in a warmed serving dish.

Add the Grand Marnier and brandy to the skillet, heat gently and ignite. Pour the flaming liquid over the crêpes and serve immediately.
Serves 4

Crêpes au Chocolat

BATTER:
1 cup all-purpose
   flour
pinch of salt
2 tablespoons sugar
1 tablespoon instant
   coffee
1 tablespoon
   unsweetened cocoa
2 eggs, beaten
1¼ cups milk
1 tablespoon oil
CHOCOLATE SAUCE:
6 squares (1 oz each)
   semi-sweet
   chocolate
⅔ cup water
1 teaspoon instant
   coffee
½ cup sugar
FILLING:
1½ cups heavy
   cream
¼ cup sugar
2 tablespoons rum

Make and cook the crêpes as for
Crêpes Suzette (see opposite), sifting
the sugar, coffee and cocoa with the
flour and salt; set aside to cool.

To make the sauce, place the
chocolate, 2 tablespoons of the water
and the coffee in a small saucepan
and heat gently until melted. Add the
remaining water and the sugar and
heat gently, stirring, until dissolved.
Simmer, uncovered, for 10 minutes.
Let cool.

To make the filling, whip the
cream until fairly stiff. Fold in the
sugar and rum.

Place a tablespoon of cream on
each crêpe, roll up and place on a
serving plate. Just before serving,
pour a little chocolate sauce over.
Serve the remaining sauce separately.
Serves 6

Raspberry Gâteau

3 eggs, separated
1/2 cup sugar
grated rind and juice
of 1/2 lemon
1/2 cup all-purpose
flour, sifted
1/4 cup ground
almonds
TO FINISH:
1 1/2 cups heavy
cream, whipped
with 1/4 cup sugar
1/2 pint raspberries
1/4 cup red currant
jelly
2 teaspoons water
1/2 cup toasted
chopped almonds

Beat the egg yolks with the sugar
and lemon rind and juice until thick.
Stir in the flour and ground almonds.
Beat the egg whites until stiff and
fold into the mixture.

Pour into a greased and floured 8
inch cake pan. Bake in a preheated
350°F oven for 35 to 40 minutes.
Invert onto a wire rack to cool.

Split the cake into two layers.
Spread half the whipped cream
between the layers. Arrange the
raspberries on the top, leaving a
border around the edge.

Heat the jelly with the water and
use to brush the raspberries and the
side of the cake. Press the almonds
around the side of the cake. Pipe the
remaining whipped cream around
the top edge.
Serves 6

Strawberry Pastry Ring

CHOUX PASTRY:
4 tablespoons butter
or margarine
3/4 cup water
3/4 cup all-purpose
flour, sifted
2 eggs, beaten
1/4 cup sliced almonds
FILLING:
2 tablespoons sugar
1 pint strawberries,
halved
1 1/2 cups heavy
cream, whipped
confectioners sugar
for sprinkling

Make the choux pastry as for
Profiteroles (see opposite). Pipe onto
a dampened cookie sheet into an 8
inch ring. Sprinkle with the almonds
and bake in a preheated 425°F oven
for 15 minutes. Lower the heat to
375°F and bake for 20 to 25 minutes
longer or until golden brown. Cool
on a wire rack.

Fold the sugar and half the
strawberries into the whipped cream.

Split the ring in half horizontally
and spoon the filling into the bottom
half. Cover with the remaining
strawberries, then replace the top
half of the ring. Sprinkle with
confectioners sugar.
Serves 6

Profiteroles

CHOUX PASTRY:
4 tablespoons butter
  or margarine
3/4 cup water
3/4 cup all-purpose
  flour, sifted
2 eggs, beaten
CHOCOLATE SAUCE:
6 squares (1 oz each)
  semi-sweet
  chocolate
2/3 cup water
1 teaspoon instant
  coffee
1/2 cup sugar
FILLING:
2 tablespoons
  confectioners sugar
1/8 teaspoon vanilla
1 cup heavy cream,
  whipped

Melt the butter in a small saucepan, add the water and bring to a boil. Add the flour all at once and beat until the mixture leaves the side of the pan. Cool, then add the eggs a little at a time, beating vigorously.

Spoon the dough into a pastry bag fitted with a plain 1/2 inch tip and pipe small mounds onto a dampened cookie sheet.

Bake in a preheated 425°F oven for 10 minutes, then lower the heat to 375°F and bake for 20 to 25 minutes longer or until golden. Make a slit in the side of each round. Cool on a wire rack.

Make the chocolate sauce as for Crêpes au Chocolat (see page 79).

To make the filling, fold the sugar and vanilla into the whipped cream. Pipe or spoon a little filling into each profiterole. Arrange the profiteroles on a serving dish. Pour the chocolate sauce over.

Serves 4 to 6

Strawberry Shortbread

½ cup butter
¼ cup sugar
1 cup all-purpose
   flour, sifted
½ cup cornstarch
½ pint strawberries
1½ cups heavy
   cream, whipped
   with ¼ cup sugar
confectioners sugar
   for sprinkling

Cream the butter and sugar together until soft, then stir in the flour and cornstarch. Mix to a firm dough, then place on a floured surface and knead lightly. Divide the dough in half. Roll out each piece into an 8 inch round on a cookie sheet.

Bake in a preheated 350°F oven for 20 minutes. Let stand for a few minutes, then score one round into six sections. Carefully slide both rounds onto a wire rack to cool.

Set aside three whole strawberries for decoration; slice the remainder. Combine three-quarters of the whipped cream with the sliced strawberries and spread over the plain round of shortbread. Break the other round into sections and place on top. Sprinkle with confectioners sugar. Pipe a whipped cream rosette on each section and decorate with the reserved strawberries.
Serves 6

Hazelnut Meringue

4 egg whites
1 cup + 2
 tablespoons sugar
⅛ teaspoon vanilla
1 teaspoon vinegar
1 cup ground toasted
 hazelnuts

FILLING:
1½ cups heavy
 cream, whipped
2 tablespoons sugar
½ pint raspberries
confectioners sugar
 for sprinkling

Beat the egg whites until stiff, then beat in the sugar, a little at a time. Continue beating until the meringue is very stiff and holds its shape. Carefully fold in the vanilla, vinegar and hazelnuts.

Divide the mixture between two greased 8 inch layer cake pans and spread evenly. Bake in a preheated 350°F oven for 40 to 45 minutes or until set and lightly browned.

Run the tip of a sharp knife around the inside of the pans. Invert onto a wire rack to cool.

To make the filling, combine two-thirds of the whipped cream with the sugar and raspberries, reserving a few for decoration. Spread the filling between the layers and sprinkle the top with confectioners sugar.

Decorate with the remaining whipped cream, piped in rosettes, and the reserved raspberries.
Serves 6

Chestnut Vacherin

5 egg whites
1¼ cups sugar
FILLING:
2 cups heavy cream,
  whipped
1 can (8 oz)
  sweetened chestnut
  purée
2 tablespoons brandy
TO DECORATE:
confectioners sugar
grated chocolate

Beat the egg whites until stiff, then beat in 3 tablespoons of the sugar. Carefully fold in the remaining sugar.

Put the meringue into a pastry bag fitted with a ½ inch plain tip. Pipe into three 8 inch rounds on cookie sheets lined with parchment paper. Bake in a preheated 275°F oven for 1½ to 2 hours. Peel off the paper and cool on a wire rack.

Combine three-quarters of the whipped cream with the chestnut purée and brandy. Spread the filling between the layers.

Sprinkle with confectioners sugar and grated chocolate. Pipe the remaining whipped cream around the edge.

Serves 8

Meringue Baskets

MERINGUE:
4 egg whites
1/8 teaspoon vanilla
2 1/4 cups
  confectioners sugar
FILLING:
3/4 cup heavy cream,
  whipped
1/2 pint strawberries
2 tablespoons red
  currant jelly,
  warmed

Beat the egg whites until stiff, then beat in the vanilla and the confectioners sugar, a little at a time. Continue beating until the meringue is very stiff.

Line a cookie sheet with parchment paper and draw eight 3 inch circles on the paper. Spread half the meringue over the circles to form bases. Put the remaining meringue into a pastry bag fitted with a large fluted tip and pipe around the edge of each base.

Bake in a preheated 300°F oven for 1 to 1 1/4 hours. Cool on a wire rack. Remove the paper.

Spoon a little whipped cream into each basket and arrange the strawberries on top. Brush the red currant jelly over the strawberries to glaze.

Makes 8

Black Forest Gâteau

SPONGE MIXTURE:
3 large eggs
1/2 cup sugar
1/2 cup all-purpose flour
2 tablespoons unsweetened cocoa
1 tablespoon oil
TO FINISH:
1 can (16 oz) pitted, dark sweet cherries
1 tablespoon arrowroot
1/4 cup Kirsch
1 1/2 cups heavy cream, whipped with 1/4 cup sugar
chocolate curls (see page 65)

Beat the eggs and sugar together in a bowl until thick. Sift the flour with the cocoa and fold into the egg mixture with the oil.

Pour into a greased 8 inch cake pan. Bake in a preheated 375°F oven for 30 to 35 minutes or until the cake springs back when lightly pressed. Invert onto a wire rack to cool.

Drain the cherries, reserving the juice. Mix a little of the juice with the arrowroot in a small bowl. Pour the remaining juice into a saucepan and bring to a boil. Pour into the arrowroot and stir well. Return to the pan and heat gently, stirring, until thick and clear. Add the cherries and let cool.

Slice the cake into two layers and sprinkle both layers with Kirsch. Place one layer on a plate, and pipe a line of cream around the top. Spread the cherry mixture in the center and place the second layer on top.

Spread half the remaining whipped cream around the side of the cake and press chocolate curls into it. Pipe the remaining whipped cream on top.
Serves 6

Crème Brûlée

4 egg yolks
2 tablespoons sugar
2½ cups heavy
   cream
¼ teaspoon vanilla
TO FINISH:
¼ cup sugar

Beat the egg yolks and sugar together. Warm the cream in the top of a double boiler over simmering water. Carefully stir in the egg mixture. Continue cooking gently, stirring constantly, until thick enough to coat the back of a spoon. Add the vanilla.

Strain into six ramekins and place in a roasting pan containing 1 inch water. Bake in a preheated 275°F oven for 30 to 40 minutes.

Remove the dishes from the pan. Cool, then chill overnight.

To finish, sprinkle the sugar over the tops. Place under a preheated broiler and cook until the sugar has caramelized. Cool, then chill for 2 hours before serving.

Serves 6

Strawberry Mille Feuille

1 sheet (½ of a
   17¼ oz pkg)
   frozen puff pastry,
   thawed
1 pint strawberries
¼ cup confectioners
   sugar
1½ cups heavy cream,
   whipped
¼ cup red currant
   jelly
2 teaspoons water
¼ cup chopped
   toasted almonds

Cut the pastry dough into 3 pieces and roll out each into a 5 × 12 inch rectangle. Place on cookie sheets, prick all over and chill for 15 minutes.

Bake in a preheated 425°F oven for 10 to 12 minutes or until golden brown. Cool on a wire rack. Trim the edges to make them even; crumble the trimmings and reserve.

Coarsely chop half the strawberries; cut the remainder in half and set aside. Fold the chopped strawberries and confectioners sugar into the whipped cream. Spread half the strawberry mixture on one piece of pastry. Place a second layer of pastry on top and spread with the remaining strawberry mixture. Top with the last piece of pastry.

Heat the red currant jelly with the water. Brush the top pastry layer with this glaze and arrange the remaining strawberries on top. Brush with the glaze. Combine the crumbled pastry with the almonds and press against the sides.
Serves 8

Crumb-Topped Cheesecake

6 tablespoons butter
    or margarine
2½ cups graham
    cracker crumbs
⅓ cup firmly packed
    brown sugar
1½ cups cream-style
    cottage cheese
¼ cup sugar
3 eggs, separated
grated rind of 1
    lemon
2 envelopes (2
    tablespoons)
    unflavored gelatin,
    soaked in ¼ cup
    water
2 cups heavy cream,
    whipped

Melt the butter in a saucepan. Mix in the crumbs and brown sugar. Spread half the mixture in the bottom of an 8 inch loose-bottomed cake pan and chill until firm.

Place the cottage cheese in a bowl and beat in the sugar, egg yolks and lemon rind. Put the gelatin mixture in a bowl over a pan of simmering water and stir until dissolved, then stir into the cheese mixture.

Fold two-thirds of the whipped cream into the cheese mixture. Beat the egg whites until stiff and fold into the mixture. Spoon on top of the crumb crust and chill for 10 minutes. Sprinkle the remaining crumb mixture over the top of the filling and chill for 2 hours.

Remove the cheesecake from the pan and decorate with the remaining whipped cream.
Serves 8

Walnut Meringue Gâteau

MERINGUE:
4 egg whites
1 cup sugar
*½ cup ground
walnuts*

FILLING:
½ cup sugar
¼ cup water
*¼ cup hot black
coffee*
*2 cups heavy cream,
whipped*

TO FINISH:
confectioners sugar
8 walnut halves

Beat the egg whites until stiff, then beat in 2 tablespoons of the sugar. Carefully fold in the remaining sugar with the ground walnuts.

Put the meringue into a pastry bag fitted with a ½ inch plain tip and pipe into two 8 inch rounds on cookie sheets lined with parchment paper. Bake in a preheated 275°F oven for 1½ to 2 hours. Transfer to a wire rack to cool.

Place the sugar and water in a saucepan and heat gently until dissolved. Increase the heat and cook to a rich brown caramel. Remove from the heat, carefully add the coffee and stir until the caramel has melted, heating again if necessary. Let cool.

Fold the whipped cream into the caramel and spread three-quarters between the meringue layers. Sprinkle the top with confectioners sugar. Pipe cream around the edge and decorate with walnut halves.
Serves 6

Hazelnut and Apple Shortbread

HAZELNUT PASTRY:
*6 tablespoons butter
   or margarine*
¼ cup sugar
*1 cup all-purpose
   flour, sifted*
*¾ cup ground toasted
   hazelnuts*

FILLING:
*1 tablespoon apricot
   jam*
*1 lb apples, peeled,
   cored and sliced*
¼ cup raisins
¼ cup currants
*1 teaspoon apple pie
   spice*
*¾ cup heavy cream,
   whipped*

TO FINISH:
*confectioners sugar
8 hazelnuts*

Cream the butter and sugar together until light and fluffy. Stir in the flour and ground hazelnuts and mix to a firm dough. Knead on a floured surface until smooth. Divide in half and roll out each piece into an 8 inch round on a cookie sheet.

Bake in a preheated 375°F oven for 15 to 20 minutes. Cut one round into 8 sections while still warm. Place both rounds on a wire rack to cool.

Place the jam and apples in a saucepan, cover and cook gently for 15 to 20 minutes or until softened, stirring occasionally. Add the raisins, currants and spice. Let cool.

Spread the apple mixture over the hazelnut round. Cover with half the whipped cream. Arrange the hazelnut sections on top and sprinkle with confectioners sugar. Pipe a rosette of whipped cream on each section and top with hazelnuts.
Serves 8

91

Apple Crêpe Cake

CRÊPES:
1 cup all-purpose
    flour
pinch of salt
1 egg, beaten
1½ cups milk
1 tablespoon oil

FILLING:
2 tablespoons butter
    or margarine
1½ lb apples, peeled,
    cored and sliced
⅓ cup firmly packed
    brown sugar
¼ teaspoon ground
    cinnamon
¼ teaspoon ground
    cloves
½ cup golden raisins

TO FINISH:
¼ cup apricot jam,
    warmed
¼ cup toasted sliced
    almonds

Make and cook the crêpes as for Crêpes Suzette (see page 78).

Melt the butter in a saucepan. Add the apples, sugar, cinnamon, cloves and raisins. Cover and simmer for 10 to 15 minutes or until the apples are tender.

Place a crêpe on a greased ovenproof plate, cover with some of the apple mixture, then another crêpe. Continue in this way until the apple mixture and crêpes are all used, finishing with a crêpe.

Spoon the apricot jam over to glaze. Bake in a preheated 350°F oven for 10 to 15 minutes or until heated through.

Cut into wedges and sprinkle with almonds. Serve with whipped cream if desired.

Serves 6

Chocolate Mocha Roll

6 squares (1 oz each)
  semi-sweet
  chocolate
3 tablespoons water
1 tablespoon instant
  coffee
5 eggs, separated
1 cup sugar
confectioners sugar
  for sprinkling
FILLING:
1 tablespoon instant
  coffee
1 tablespoon boiling
  water
1½ cups heavy
  cream, whipped
2 tablespoons
  confectioners sugar

Place the chocolate, water and coffee in a saucepan and heat gently until the chocolate has melted. Remove from the heat. Beat the egg yolks with the sugar until thick and creamy, then fold in the warm chocolate mixture.

Beat the egg whites until stiff and fold into the chocolate mixture. Pour into a lined and greased 9 × 13 inch baking pan. Bake in a preheated 350°F oven for 20 to 25 minutes or until firm.

Let cool in the pan for 5 minutes, then cover with a clean damp cloth. Refrigerate overnight.

Carefully remove the cloth and turn the cake out onto a sheet of waxed paper heavily sprinkled with confectioners sugar. Peel off the lining paper.

Dissolve the coffee in the water, cool, then fold into the whipped cream with the sugar. Spread over the cake and roll up like a jelly roll. Place on a serving platter.
Serves 8

INDEX

Apple:
  Apple amber 13
  Apple crêpe cake 92
  Apple mold 10
  Apple pudding 70
  Apple snow 11
  Baked apples with dates 12
  Blackberry and apple layers 74
  Calvados apples 14
  Crisp apple bake 73
  Deep-dish apple pie 58
  French apple tart 59
  Hazelnut and apple shortbread 91
  Rhubarb and apple crumble 68
Apricot ambrosia 40
Apricot delight 10
Apricot upside-down cake 72
Avocado ice cream 55

Baked apples with dates 12
Banana:
  Banana ice 45
  Banana whip 33
  Caribbean bananas 7
Biscuit Tortoni 48
Black Forest gâteau 86
Blackberry:
  Blackberry and apple layers 74
  Blackberry ice cream 49
  Peaches in blackberry sauce 8
Blueberry pie 62
Bombe au chocolat 51
Bombe Grande Marnier 54
Bombe noël 47
Brandy butter 75
Bread and butter pudding 69
Bread pudding, raisin 66

Calvados apples 14
Caribbean bananas 7
Charlotte russe 28
Cheesecakes 64-5
Chestnut vacherin 84
Chocolate:
  Bombe au chocolat 51

Chocolate and almond mold 26
Chocolate cheesecake 65
Chocolate ice cream 44
Chocolate mocha roll 93
Chocolate and orange mousse 25
Crêpes au chocolat 79
Pots de chocolat 38
Rich chocolate mousse 22
Steamed chocolate pudding 71
Zucotto 77
Christmas pudding 74
Coffee. See also Mocha
  Coffee ice cream 44
  Mousse brazilienne 26
Creamy rice pudding 34
Crème brûlée 87
Crème caramel 40
Crémets 15
Crêpes:
  Apple crêpe cake 92
  Crêpes au chocolat 79
  Crêpes Suzette 78

Deep-dish apple pie 58

French apple tart 59
Frozen desserts 42-55
Fruit. See also Apple etc.
  Fruit chartreuse 17
  Fruit tart 63
  Red fruit compôte 14
  Tropical fruit salad 6
  Winter fruit salad 16

Gâteaux:
  Black Forest gâteau 86
  Malakoff gâteau 76
  Raspberry gâteau 80
  Walnut meringue gâteau 90
Ginger ice cream 44
Gooseberry fool 32

Hazelnut and apple shortbread 91
Hazelnut meringue 83
Honey lemon tart 56

Ice creams and Frozen Desserts 42-55
Indian pudding 67

Lemon:
  Lemon meringue pie 57
  Lemon pudding 68

INDEX

Apple:
Apple and date steamed
pudding 77
Apple meringue 78
Baked apples 70
Rhubarb and apple cobbler 72

Banana splits 67
Beef:
Beef, pepper and mushroom
casserole 32
Marinated beef kabobs 28
Shepherds' pie 34
Spaghetti Bolognaise 30
Swiss steak 29
Winter family casserole 34
Biscuits:
Cheese and ham biscuits 93
Raisin biscuits 92
Bread:
Crusty rolls 90
Farmhouse bread 90
Whole wheat bread 91
Bread pudding 76
Butterfly cakes 87

Cabbage, carrot and apple salad
52
Cakes:
Chocolate and pineapple
upside-down cake 79
Moist fruit cake 84
No-bake chocolate cake 84
Victoria layer cake 86
Carrot and orange soup 6
Carrots, glazed 45
Casseroles:
Beef, pepper and mushroom
casserole 32
Layered fish casserole 26
Liver and tomato casserole 35
Winter family casserole 34
Cauliflower:
Cauliflower, mushroom and
onion salad 56
Creamed cauliflower 48
Savory cauliflower cheese 46
Chicken:
Chicken and raisin casserole 43

Chicken liver pâté 16
Chicken pie 41
Mustard-glazed chicken 42
Orange-baked chicken 42
Southern-fried chicken 40
Chocolate and pineapple upside-
down cake 79
Clam appetizer, Hot 15
Cocoa cookies 81
Cod:
Cheesy cod 19
Cod with mushrooms 25
Cookies:
Cocoa cookies 81
Jam faces 82
Shortbread 83
Cucumber soup, cold 7

Deviled ham dip 16

Fish. *See also* cod etc.
Baked fish in cider 26
Fish and potato pie 20
Flounder with spinach 25
Kedgeree 22
Layered fish casserole 26
Smoked fish with corn 21
Fluffy orange pudding 68
French dressing 57
French onion soup 12
Fruit gelatin, layered 68
Fruit salad, family 66

Ginger layer dessert 74
Ginger gooseberry pudding 74
Grape and orange salad with
ham 52

Hamburgers 59
Honey gingerbread 88
Hot clam appetizer 15

Irish stew 30

Jam faces 82

Kedgeree 22
Kidney beans and ham 38

Lamb:
Irish stew 30
Meat pancakes 36
Rib lamb chops with tomatoes
and mint 37
Shepherds' pie 34